SMELL, THE SUBTLE SENSE

SMELL, THE SUBTLE SENSE

ALVIN, VIRGINIA, AND ROBERT SILVERSTEIN

ILLUSTRATED BY
ANN NEUMANN

MORROW JUNIOR BOOKS   New York

Printed in the United States of America.
Design by Trish Parcell Watts
1   2   3   4   5   6   7   8   9   10

Library of Congress Cataloging-in-Publication Data
Silverstein, Alvin.
Smell : the subtle sense / Alvin, Virginia, and Robert Silverstein ; illustrated by Ann Neumann.
p.   cm.
Includes index.
Summary: Discusses the complex nature of the sense of smell and
the importance of the nose. Also discusses how odors are produced,
how they help in identifying specific diseases, and their
psychological and physical effects.
ISBN 0-688-09396-5 (trade)—ISBN 0-688-09397-3 (lib. bdg.)
1. Smell—Juvenile literature.   [1. Smell.   2. Senses and
sensation.   3. Nose.]   I. Silverstein, Virginia B.
II. Silverstein, Robert A.   III. Neumann, Ann, ill.   IV. Title.
QP458.S56   1992
612.8'6—dc20   91-21745   CIP   AC

Contents

The World of Smell

Do you notice something odd about the faces in the picture across from this page—something missing? Of course, it is quite obvious—it's as plain as the nose on your face!

What would life be like if, like those people in the picture, you didn't have a nose? Breathing would be rather difficult: You would have to keep your mouth open and breathe in and out through it, as you do when your nose is stopped up by a cold. And you would not be able to smell anything. That might seem like an advantage sometimes, when there is a bad smell around. But you would also miss the delicious odor of a cake baking in the oven, the fragrance of a rose, the tang of spices, and the fresh smell of a just-mowed lawn. (And even being able to detect unpleasant smells can be useful, if it saves you from eating spoiled food or warns of escaping gas.)

The nose is a double-duty organ: It is part of the system for breathing, and it is also a sense organ that gathers information about smells.

People's noses come in a variety of shapes and sizes, but they are all equipped to do their breathing and smelling jobs. In the animal world there is even more variety. Some animals have noses that are pretty much like ours, though they may be much more sensitive to smells. But other animals do not have an organ that could really be called a nose. They manage the tasks of breathing and detecting odors with quite different structures— perhaps by breathing through holes in their bodies and smelling with antennae on top of their heads or even with their feet!

Smells, too, vary greatly, and they have a number of uses in the living world. The sweet smells of plants are part of a working

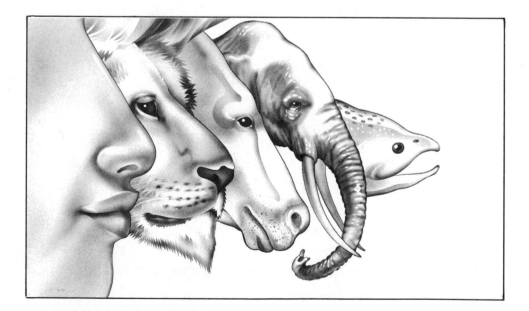

partnership between plants and animals: Plants provide food for insects, bats, and other creatures, and animals help pollinate the flowers or spread the seeds to provide for the new plant generation. Animals use smells to communicate with others of their kind—to find mates and mark trails and territories. Humans produce smells, too, but instead of using them we often act as though we were ashamed of them. We wash them away with soaps or cover them up with perfumes.

We are rarely conscious of the smells in our world unless they are unusually intense, or pleasant, or unpleasant. But they have a deep emotional effect and are often linked with our strongest and most long-lasting memories.

In this book we'll explore the world of smell—the subtlest and most neglected of all our senses—and its meaning in our lives and those of the other creatures of our planet.

1

Kinds of Smells

Smell is one of the simplest senses. It is a chemical sense—we perceive odors when tiny, microscopic particles floating through the air react chemically with special sensory cells in the lining of our noses. In fact, just a few molecules—the tiniest units of the odor-producing chemicals—may be enough to trigger a smell.

For many living creatures, smell or similar chemical senses are extremely important for survival, but we humans depend far more on our senses of sight and hearing. Although the link between an odor and the brain is one of the most direct, people usually find smell a fuzzy sense, difficult to describe.

Humans can detect about ten thousand different smells. But when most people sniff a sampling of odors without seeing what is producing them, they may not be able to identify many of the smells. For some reason, they just can't make the connection, although the smell may seem familiar. And yet, we tend to remember smells and recognize them when we meet them again (even if we can't identify them in words).

Our senses allow us to experience the world around us. We can put into words descriptions of the things we experience with all our senses—except the sense of smell. We see colors like red, blue, and yellow. We hear words that we can break into consonants and vowels, and music that we can break into individual musical notes. We can taste sweet, bitter, sour, and salty; and we can feel rough, smooth, jagged, and bumpy. But there is no way to describe a smell without using the name of the thing that is being smelled or comparing it to another smell. Something smells like rotten eggs, or like flowers, but what do those scents smell like?

Classifying Smells

The sense of smell has always been the least understood sense. The ancient Greek philosopher Plato divided smells into pleasant ones and unpleasant ones. Yet people differ greatly in their reactions to smells. One person may find the odor of frying eggs delicious, while another finds the same odor disgusting. Reactions toward smells also seem to vary with age and sex. One study showed that up to the age of about eight, the favorite odor of both boys and girls is strawberry, and both dislike oily smells. Between eight and fourteen, boys like the smell of orange blossoms, while girls like the tarlike smell of naphthalene. Between fifteen and nineteen, lavender becomes a popular scent, especially for boys, and strawberry has lost much of its charm for both sexes. Young women prefer the scents of lavender and almond, while musk and orange blossoms are the favorites of young men.

As you will see later, reactions to smells have also been found to be influenced by time of day and past experiences.

Aristotle, another famous Greek philosopher, declared that if something smelled good, it was good for us, and if it smelled bad, it was bad for us. He believed that smell was very similar to taste and classified odors as sweet, bitter, pungent, sour, harsh, and succulent.

The Swedish naturalist Carolus Linnaeus proposed a classification system for smells about two thousand years later, in 1752. He divided smells into seven classes: (1) aromatic; (2) fragrant; (3) ambrosial (musky); (4) alliaceous (garlicky); (5) hycrine (goaty or cheesy); (6) repulsive; and (7) nauseous.

The next smell landmark was a book called *The Physiology of Smell,* published in 1895. In it, Dutch physiologist Hendrik Zwaardemaker divided odors into nine classes. He based his classification system on the work of Linnaeus, as well as on discoveries in the rapidly developing field of chemistry. According to Zwaardemaker, the types of smells are:

1. ethereal (fruits, ethers, resins)
2. aromatic (aniseed, almond, camphor, cloves, lavender, lemon)
3. fragrant (flowers, vanilla)
4. ambrosial (amber, musk)
5. alliaceous (onions, garlic, hydrogen sulfide, chlorine)
6. empyreumatic (roasted coffee, tobacco smoke, burned animal or plant substances)

7. caprillic (cheese, sweat, rancid fat)
8. repulsive (narcotics, nightshade, bedbugs)
9. nauseating (rotting flesh, excrement)

Zwaardemaker claimed that the first four classes were pleasant smells for humans, whereas the last four were not. Alliaceous smells were unpleasant for some but pleasant for others. (However, today many people would find empyreumatic smells like roasted coffee or burning leaves pleasant—which just goes to show how subjective reactions to smells can be.) This classification of smells was highly regarded in smell research for many years.

In 1916 German psychologist Hans Henning made another important contribution to the study of smell when he devised a six-class scheme: (1) fragrant; (2) ethereal or fruity; (3) resinous; (4) spicy; (5) putrid; (6) burned. He designed a three-dimensional five-sided prism with each joining corner assigned to one of the six classes. Henning believed that all odors were related and that a particular odor fell somewhere between two corners, or classes. For example, vanilla fell on the face between fragrant and spicy but was much closer to fragrant. Clove, on the same face, was closer to spicy.

Smell researchers found this system useful, but many smells did not seem to fit the model. Also, when different people smelled the same odor, their reactions to it varied. They might each put the same odor on different sides of the prism.

Modern researchers have found more important distinctions among kinds of smells. For example, most organic substances (compounds that contain carbon and are found in or produced by living things) have odors, but we can't smell many nonorganic

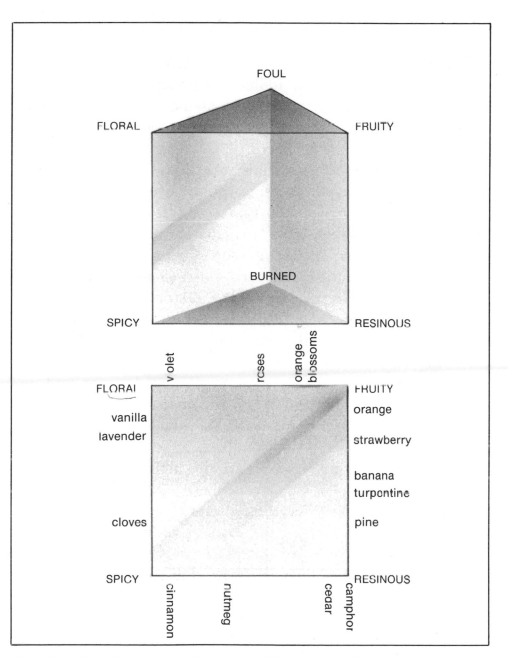

Hans Henning plotted odors along a five-sided prism with six corners. A sample plot for one side shows the positions of some common odors.

materials. Some of the ones we can smell are elements such as bromine, chlorine, fluorine, iodine, and phosphorus. We can also smell such nonorganic compounds as ammonia, hydrogen sulfide (the "rotten egg" smell), nitrogen oxide, ozone, and sulfur dioxide.

Most of these nonorganic substances have unpleasant smells. Some of them are irritating and cause the eyes and nose to run. This effect is called *trigeminal stimulation*. It is the body's warning signal that these things are potentially harmful and we should stay away from them. The recognition of certain smells as danger signals is partly learned and partly instinctive—reinforced by millions of years of experience. Our ancestors who avoided dangerous things with strong, distinctive odors were the ones who survived, and they passed this sensory reaction down to us.

Rotting carcasses and feces give off odors of ammonia, hydrogen sulfide, and various other smells that humans find unpleasant. We tend to avoid them, and that is a useful survival trait. The bacteria that break down the bodies of dead animals produce toxins that could poison us.

Rotting food and body wastes are not harmful to all animals, though. Some animal scavengers actually feed on decaying matter. (Their bodies can change the bacterial toxins into harmless substances.) For these animals, the smells of decay are attractive. The smell of feces or rotting carcasses draws insects like ants, flies, and beetles. They feed on the dead matter or lay their eggs in it. The turkey vulture, a scavenging bird, has a much keener sense of smell than most birds. It can sniff out the difference between a fresh carcass and one that has been decaying too long. Turkey vultures have been known to circle around leaking gas lines because they smell the ethyl mercaptan that has been added to the gas to make it an unpleasant warning signal for humans.

Another way of classifying smells is by their associations with experiences that many people share. The smell of buttered popcorn may register in our minds as a "movie smell." There are also typical hospital smells, school smells, laboratory smells, and church smells.

In the mid-1970s, a U.S. Department of Agriculture researcher, John Amoore, came up with a new classification theory. He believes that there are basic or "primary" odors, much like the primary colors (red, blue, and yellow) or tastes (sweet, sour, bitter, and salty). Dr. Amoore says that the odors we recognize are combinations of at least thirty primary odors. He has isolated four of them. Three of these compounds (isovaleric acid, 1-pyrroline, and trimethylamine) are believed to be sex attractants, or chemicals produced by animals that make them appealing to members of the opposite sex. (Oddly enough, these chemicals by themselves have odors that most people find unpleasant—isovaleric acid smells like rancid cheese, 1-pyrroline has a sharp ammonia odor, and trimethylamine smells fishy.) The fourth primary odor (isobutyraldehyde) is found in foods and smells like malt. Dr. Amoore believes that the primary odors may provide important information about foods, places, dangers, and members of the opposite sex.

What Smells Have in Common

If a bottle of ionone (a synthetic chemical with the odor of violets) were poured out over home plate in the Houston Astrodome, after a while the fans in the farthest parts of the stands would be smelling violets—even though there are no winds to carry the scent inside the domed stadium.

How is this possible? It happens because, although we can't see air, it is not just empty space. Our atmosphere is made up of gas particles, too small to be seen. Each of these tiny particles is in constant motion, and from time to time they bump into other particles, bouncing off each other like microscopic Ping-Pong balls. It is these bouncing air molecules that spread the odor particles through the air and carry them from one place to another.

Ionone is a liquid, but like other odor-producing substances, it is rather volatile. This means that molecules of ionone are

Constantly moving gas molecules spread odors through the air.

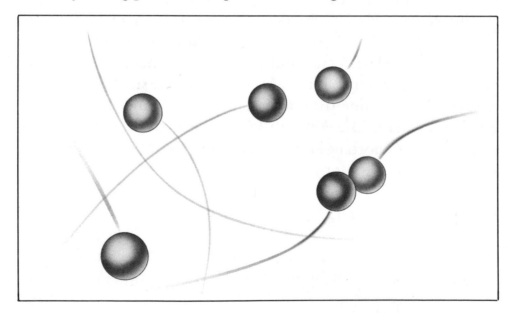

constantly leaving its surface and floating off into the air. At room temperature we cannot smell iron, steel, and many other common substances because they are not volatile and thus do not send particles into the air to be carried to our noses. On the other hand, our noses can detect some odor-producing substances very readily. Humans can smell vanilla when two-millionths of a milligram of it is present in a cubic millimeter of air; a single molecule of green pepper odor can be detected when it is diluted with a trillion molecules of air. These are extraordinarily tiny amounts!

Odors generally get stronger as the temperature rises. When substances are warmed, they become more volatile, as well as more aromatic, because the particles are moving faster and faster and bouncing into each other more frequently.

An odor would not be a smell without some means of smelling it. We humans have a specialized smelling organ, the nose. Many animals have noses rather similar to ours, but others use a variety of different—but effective—smelling devices, as you will see in the next chapter.

2

All Kinds of Noses

The sense of smell must have arisen very early in the history of life on our planet. Nearly every form of life uses chemical senses to one degree or another. Even single-celled creatures like the ameba use chemical cues, carried to them by molecules of substances dissolved in the water, to find food and to avoid danger.

Insect "Noses"

Among the insects, which make up the largest group of animals on earth, smell is a very important sense. But insects do not have a "nose" like ours. Their smell organs are in different locations.

The gypsy moth, for instance, has special sensory cells on each of its two featherlike antennae. Altogether, they have about one hundred thousand cells (compared to fifty million in the human nose). In the male gypsy moth, half of these sensory cells detect odors that bring in a wide variety of information about the world. Each of these cells is sensitive to one type of odor. The other half of the sensors all respond to a single kind of smell information: the scents produced by the female gypsy moth. If the wind is right, a male gypsy moth can pick up the scent of a female several miles away. The male silkworm moth, with an even more powerful sense of smell, can detect a female seven miles away. One scientist calculated that if a bucketful of the female scent, a chemical called bombykol, were poured into the oceans of the earth and diluted in all of that water, there would be enough

The gypsy moth smells with specialized sensory cells on its antennae.

molecules in any single thimbleful of seawater to excite a male.

Insects' smell organs are also an important means of finding food. The fragrance of flowers can attract bees for miles around. The smell tells the bee where to find a source of nectar to sip and pollen to carry back to the hive. Mosquitoes find their animal food sources by detecting exhaled carbon dioxide. Then they zero in to suck up a meal of blood. Tsetse flies can pick up the breath of a cow from many miles away.

Insects' antennae and legs are covered with tiny bristles. The bristles that are used for smelling are hollowed out inside. They have many openings that permit odors to enter. At the bottom of each bristle is one or more receptor cells that are sensitive to a specific odor chemical.

Some insects and other animals have chemical sensors on their feet. Butterflies and houseflies use these sensors to tell whether they have landed on a good food source. That chemical sense is more like our sense of taste, but spiders and scorpions actually smell with their feet. Sensory cells on their first pair of walking legs act like "noses" that gather information about the environment.

"Noses" in the Water

Like insects, the animals that live in the sea also use their chemical sense to hunt for food, avoid their enemies, and find a mate. This sense could be regarded as taste, because it is stimulated by chemicals dissolved in water rather than air. But it works very much like land animals' sense of smell, bringing information by means of very tiny amounts of chemicals, sometimes carried over great distances.

Lobsters smell with their antennules, two tiny antennae protruding from their heads. They wave them constantly in the water the way elephants sniff the air with their trunks.

Starfish "noses" are sense cells located on small tentacles at the ends of their five arms. Using them, a starfish can smell a clam buried deep in the sand.

Octopuses can squirt out a fluid that blocks the sense of smell in their enemy, the moray eel. With that chemical defense floating in the water, the octopus can get away undetected. This is quite a feat, for many fish—including eels—have extremely sensitive chemical sensors. A trout can detect chemicals from a shrimp (one of its favorite food sources) diluted a billion times. And an eel's smell sense is a billion times keener than a trout's!

A salmon can smell chemicals from its birthplace hundreds of miles away. It will swim upstream, passing numerous tiny rivers and streams, until it reaches the place of its birth. In the spawning season, salmon flock in from the ocean to mate and lay eggs for the new generation. Sea turtles, too, return to their birthplace to lay eggs, using their sense of smell to help them find the way.

In fish, the smell sensory cells are found in a pair of pockets in the head. Openings in the front and rear permit water to flow over these sensory cells. The fish's nasal structures are not connected to its mouth in any way, as they are in mammals. Many fish, including the minnow, can smell with other parts of their outer skin and tail, as well. When a minnow is injured, its skin gives off a chemical that alerts all the other minnows in the area. This danger scent makes the whole school of minnows dart away from the area.

Noses on the Land

Snakes use their forked tongues to pick up scents from the air. Their tongue picks up chemicals from the air and then transfers them to a smell organ called the vomeronasal organ, or Jacobson's organ, which is located in two pockets in the roof of the mouth. (Amphibians, reptiles, and some mammals use a vomeronasal organ for smelling. A form of this organ is also present in newborn human babies, but it shrinks as they grow.)

Most birds do not have much sense of smell. Instead, they rely mainly on vision. This is a more efficient sense for the kind of information a flying bird needs. Keen vision shows it the exact position of an insect or seeds to eat, an enemy zooming in to

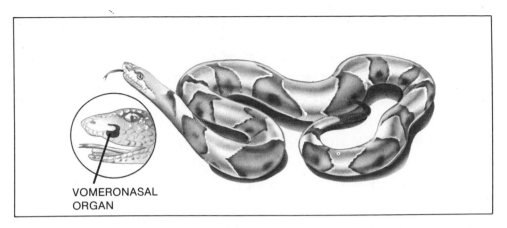

VOMERONASAL
ORGAN

A snake's forked tongue picks up odor chemicals from the air and transfers them to a smell organ in the roof of its mouth.

attack it, or the twig on a tree branch where it can land safely. Smell, on the other hand, just gives information on the direction of the source of odor chemicals, unless it is very close by.

There are some birds with a good sense of smell, however. Giant kiwis and tiny magpies can sniff out food beneath the ground, then dig down with their sharp claws to get it. The turkey vulture can detect a freshly killed carcass through miles of dense forest. Many shore birds have excellent smell senses, too, and use them to find clams and other food sources hidden in the wet sand at the sea's edge.

Like other animals, many mammals also use their sense of smell to find food. A polar bear can smell a dead seal as much as twelve miles away. Other bears that live farther south are well known for their liking of honey and their ability to sniff out the location of beehives miles from their dens. Pigs can pick up the scent of truffles growing under six inches of soil, and squirrels can find nuts they buried months before.

While an animal is eating, its sense of smell picks up aromas from the mouth cavity—the flavor of foods is actually a combination of the sense messages from the taste buds in the mouth and those from the olfactory (smell) sensors in the nose. The messages from the smell organs are sent to certain olfactory areas in the brain, where they are sorted out and interpreted. You will learn more about this in the next chapter.

The mammals that walk on all fours tend to have a very keen sense of smell. The olfactory lobes in the brain are very large, and in many of these mammals the nasal regions occupy up to half the length of the skull. Much of the space in this nasal area is for the sensory cells of smell.

The elephant's nose, in the form of a long, flexible trunk, allows it to pick up scents from down near the ground. The trunk serves double duty. It also acts as a kind of hand with which the elephant can feel things and pick them up.

In general, carnivores, or meat eaters such as tigers and lions, have the largest olfactory areas. They depend mainly on scent rather than on sight in tracking their prey. The dog, another carnivore, has a sensory area inside its nasal passages that is fifteen times as large as the olfactory area in the human nose, and its sense of smell is a million times as keen as ours. A bloodhound, the champion among dog trackers, can detect the scent from a human fingerprint made six weeks before!

A keen sense of smell is the main defense for many prey animals. The deer flares its nostrils to draw in more air and catches the scent of predators lurking upwind from it.

On the other hand, for animals that make their homes in trees, good vision is very important, but a keen sense of smell is not as useful. Like the flying birds, these animals need very exact

information about the locations of distant things. (A squirrel leaping from one branch to another needs to know more than just its general direction!) So it's not surprising that the tree-dwelling monkeys and apes, for example, do not have as keen a sense of smell as their ground-living neighbors.

When our distant ancestors came down from the trees and began to spend most of their time on the ground, they did not regain a keen sense of smell. We humans inherited a fairly good—but not great—sense of smell.

The Development of Smell as a Sense

In terms of evolution, the sense of smell was a very important development. It allowed creatures to detect things in the environment from a distance. Mobility, or the ability of creatures to move about, had enabled animals to move around in search of food. Plants and other creatures that do not move have to wait until food comes to them. Primitive creatures that developed a sense of smell had a way to point them in the direction of the food. The early fish were guided by tiny molecules and trace substances that chemically stimulated their "noses" and let them know there was food to be found. This was the first time the sense of smell was separated from the sense of taste.

The sense of smell then evolved and expanded to "sniff out" other things besides food. The animal could "smell" enemies, friends, or a mate.

The nose is only part of the story of smell. Sense messages from the nose are sent to the brain, which "makes sense" of them—and only then does an animal smell an odor.

The sense of smell was an important link in the evolution of the brain. Gary Lynch, a neurobiologist at the University of California, Irvine, believes that our fact-storing memory began in primitive mammals one hundred million years ago as a way of keeping track of odors. The odors became associated with specific things in the environment.

Eventually the tissue at the top of the nerve cord of primitive creatures that was involved in this association of smells with objects became more complex. The nerve cells began to be involved in other capacities, and a brain developed. Other brain capacities—such as the coordination of movements; the senses of hearing and sight; the ability to learn, remember, and think—began to play larger roles as the human brain evolved, and eventually the sense of smell became less important. Only a small

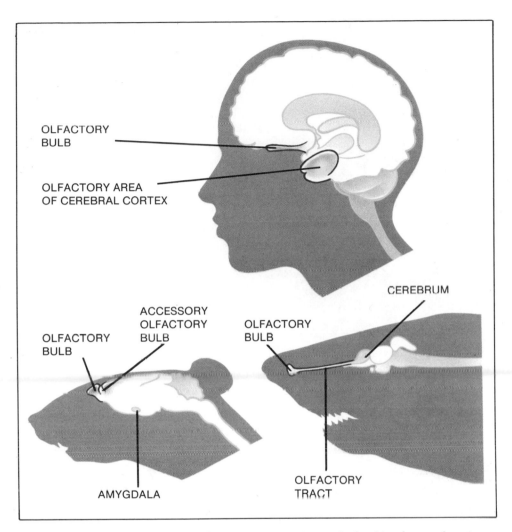

Olfactory areas in the brain (human's, mouse's, and shark's shown here) are devoted to processing odor information.

portion of the human brain is devoted to receiving and processing the smell messages from the nose. This is in sharp contrast to animals like sharks, in which the smell area takes up a large portion of the brain.

3

How We Smell

Many people feel that smell is one of our least important senses. It certainly has been one of the least understood of the senses.

The classical Greeks had several ideas about how our smell sense works. Democritus, who lived from 460 to 360 B.C., believed that tiny particles called atoms have their own individual size, shape, and texture. When they reach our noses, these atoms trigger sensations of the whole object the atoms came from.

Later in the fourth century B.C., Aristotle declared that everything in the world is composed of four elements: air, earth, fire, and water. According to this famous Greek philosopher, smell involves the element of fire. We smell things when the odor warms the body's olfactory organs.

In the second century B.C., the Greek physician Galen believed that odors go directly to the part of the brain that is involved with smell. There the odors are converted into "cerebral winds." Galen said that the brain is constantly pulsating (like the heart). With each contraction it sucks the cerebral winds into the brain cavities, then exhales the cerebral winds when it contracts.

The Renaissance brought a flood of new knowledge and experimentation in many fields, including various aspects of human anatomy and physiology. But our knowledge of smell remained in the dark ages until 1890, when the Spanish neuroanatomist Ramon y Cajal outlined the nerve pathways from the nasal lining through the olfactory bulb on the underside of the brain and on to the part of the brain concerned with smell.

As mentioned earlier, another smell pioneer was Dutch physiologist Hendrik Zwaardemaker, who published *The Physiology of Smell* in 1895. This book was the first scientific study of how we smell odors.

Since these simple beginnings, science has come a long way toward understanding this subtle sense. But there are still some questions that remain to be answered before we fully understand the sense of smell.

Your Smell Organ: the Nose

Although some people think they have a big nose, humans have much smaller noses than many other animals, such as dogs. The two nostrils lead into a pair of cavities, separated by a partition called a septum. The nasal cavities are not straight tubes. Three bony plates (the turbinates) project into each passage. They act as baffles, breaking up the flow of air and making it swirl around.

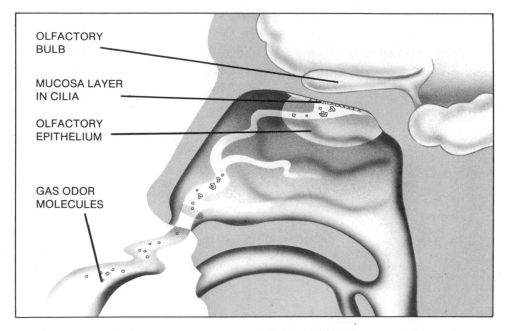

OLFACTORY
BULB

MUCOSA LAYER
IN CILIA

OLFACTORY
EPITHELIUM

GAS ODOR
MOLECULES

Air drawn into the nasal passages carries odor molecules to the sensitive olfactory membrane.

(This swirling action helps to warm the air and also brings more air particles into contact with the nasal lining.) Eventually the two nasal passages join into a common channel that leads down into the lungs.

The part of our nose that is involved with the sense of smell is actually quite small. About 95 percent of the nasal cavity has nothing to do with smell. Instead, most of the nose is involved in filtering the air we breathe so it is safe when it reaches the lungs. The nose's smell area is the olfactory membrane, two small patches of yellowish gray tissue, each about the size of a postage stamp. The olfactory membrane lines the two olfactory clefts, located beneath the bridge of the nose.

The nasal cavity is lined with a mucous membrane, covered with tiny hairlike structures called cilia. The cilia move back and forth, pushing mucus (a slimy liquid) toward the throat. The nasal membranes produce a quart of mucus each day. Dust and bacteria that enter the nose are trapped by the sticky mucus and carried down the throat and into the stomach, where they are destroyed.

In addition to protecting the body by washing away potentially harmful dust and bacteria, mucus also protects the sensitive smelling apparatus in the olfactory membrane. Mucus is also needed to carry smell particles to the olfactory membrane. In order to be detected by tiny sensory cells in the olfactory membrane, chemicals must be dissolved in a liquid. Scientists say this is a legacy from our evolutionary ancestors that lived in the sea.

When the body produces too much mucus—when we have a cold or allergies, for example—the mucus blocks the opening to the olfactory cleft, and we lose our ability to smell.

Unlike the rest of the mucous lining of the nasal cavity, the olfactory membrane contains pigment molecules, colored compounds that give it a yellowish color. Scientists are not sure exactly what the olfactory pigments do. However, they seem to play some role in smell, because albino animals, which have no pigmentation, have no sense of smell.

When we breathe, only a part of the passing air reaches the olfactory cleft. Perhaps 2 to 10 percent of the smell particles that enter the nose reach the olfactory membrane during normal breathing. When we purposely sniff something, though, much more air travels up into the cleft, increasing the proportion to 20 percent.

The Olfactory Membrane

Under an electron microscope, the olfactory membrane looks something like spaghetti in a thick, sticky sauce. The "thick sauce" is mucus, produced in the membrane. The olfactory membrane contains millions of receptor cells that are sensitive to smell. (Estimates range from ten to fifty million of them in each olfactory cleft. That seems quite impressive when we consider that up to one hundred million of these cells fit into an area the size of a postage stamp. However, German shepherds are reported to have about a *billion* receptor cells per olfactory cleft.)

The olfactory receptor cells are actually nerve cells, or neu-

This close-up of the olfactory membrane shows the dangling olfactory hairs (cilia), which pick up odor molecules.

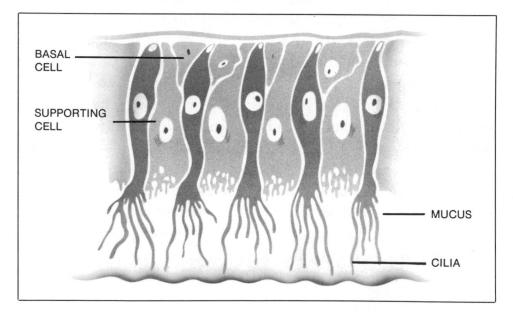

rons. Each one ends in a knob, from which six to twelve tiny olfactory hairs, or cilia, dangle into the gooey mucus. These are the "spaghetti strands" that can be seen under the electron microscope. The cilia on the olfactory receptor cells are like parts of an antenna, reaching out for smell particles. Researchers have calculated that if all the cilia in the olfactory membranes of a rabbit were spread out, they would cover an area the size of a sheet of typewriter paper! In humans the surface area of the cilia is a little less than half that size. Still, this is rather impressive since this is more than fifty times the area of the two olfactory clefts.

A thin layer of mucus, about six-hundredths of a millimeter thick, is all that protects the olfactory cilia from the outside world. This is quite remarkable when you consider that the olfactory hairs are actually extensions of the brain. Our sense of smell is the most directly brain-linked sense. The other sense organs also send their messages to the brain, but these messages must pass through numerous body structures along the way. This difference, as well as the fact that the arrangement of olfactory receptor cells and cilia is very similar throughout the animal kingdom, makes scientists believe that smell is a very old sense, evolutionarily speaking.

Skin cells are constantly exposed to the world, and they are replaced about once a month. Nerve cells, on the other hand, aren't normally regenerated when they become damaged. It is fortunate that the olfactory receptor cells are an exception to this general rule and do regenerate. Because they are in an exposed position and close to the outside world, many of these delicate nerve cells become damaged, and new cells are needed to take their place. Some researchers believe the olfactory cells become loaded with odor particles and are then disposed of like bags of garbage.

An olfactory receptor cell normally lasts about four to five weeks. New receptor cells are created in the basal layer, deep within the membrane. They move outward to the surface and soon sprout olfactory cilia. At the end of their life cycle they are broken down and flushed away by the mucus.

The Brain Link

Odor particles enter the nasal passage in the flow of inhaled air. They go up into the olfactory clefts, where they reach the olfactory membrane. To stimulate a receptor cell, an odor particle must have three important characteristics. First, it must be volatile, having readily evaporating molecules—otherwise it would never have been carried by the air into the olfactory cleft. Second, it must be at least somewhat soluble in water, so it can pass through the mucous coating to the cell. Third, it must also be fat-soluble, to penetrate into the fatty substances of the olfactory cilia.

A single cell, called a primary olfactory neuron, connects each receptor cell in the olfactory membrane to a matchhead-sized part of the brain called the olfactory bulb or olfactory lobe. There are two olfactory lobes in the brain—one for each nostril.

To reach the brain, the primary olfactory neurons must first pass through the skull. They thread their way through a penny-thin bone at the front of the cranial cavity, called the cribiform plate, which is pierced by openings like the holes in the top of a saltshaker. The olfactory bulbs rest on top of the cribiform plate.

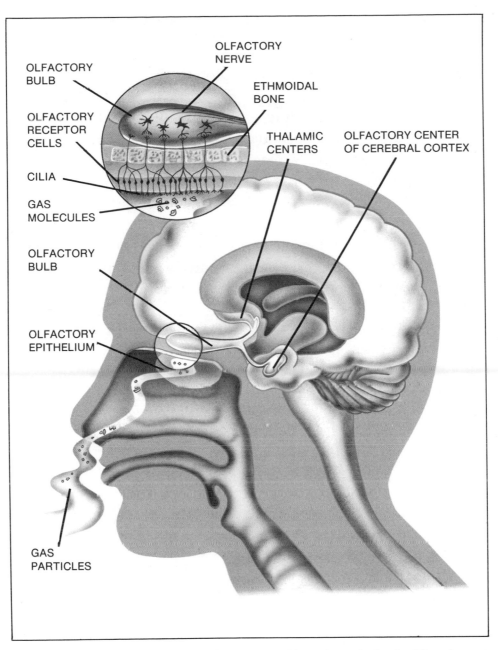

OLFACTORY
NERVE

OLFACTORY
BULB

ETHMOIDAL
BONE

OLFACTORY
RECEPTOR
CELLS

THALAMIC
CENTERS

OLFACTORY CENTER
OF CEREBRAL CORTEX

CILIA

GAS
MOLECULES

OLFACTORY
BULB

OLFACTORY
EPITHELIUM

GAS
PARTICLES

Odor messages travel from the olfactory membrane into the brain. The close-up shows the cribriform plate and synapses between neurons.

About ten million primary neurons rise up from the receptor cells and meet at structures called glomeruli. But there are only about two thousand glomeruli. Each one is like a telephone switchboard with lots of lines coming in. In the glomeruli the primary neurons meet secondary neurons. They are separated by a gap called a synapse, across which the nerve messages travel. The number of nerve messages crossing the synapse can be influenced in various ways—by hormonelike chemicals, for example—permitting fine-tuning of the sense messages.

Twenty-four secondary neurons travel from each glomerulus up a path into the brain, and another bundle of twenty-four travel over to the olfactory lobe on the other side. Since these secondary neurons are carrying the messages from five thousand primary neurons, it might seem as though a lot of information is being lost. But a nerve cell works like an electrical circuit. It can be either "on" or "off." Various combinations of "ons" and "offs" each make up a unique code, with its own special meaning. The combinations of twenty-four "ons" or "offs" can carry a huge number of different meanings, just as the twenty-six letters in the alphabet can be used to spell out any message you want to write. There can be about sixteen million different variations of on and off circuits in the two thousand glomeruli. So, theoretically, you have the capacity to distinguish sixteen million different smells.

In general, in higher animals, the peripheral nerves (the ones located outside the brain) are surrounded by a fatty covering called a myelin sheath. Like the insulation around a telephone wire, this myelin sheath shields the nerve and permits messages to flow along it more rapidly and efficiently. The olfactory neurons, though—unlike other peripheral nerves—lack a myelin sheath. Nerve messages travel much slower without this covering—an impulse moves along at the rate of only one yard per second. But there are some advantages: Because they are not coated, more nerve cells can fit into a smaller space and thus allow more information to be carried. Since lower animals typically lack myelin sheaths, their absence on the olfactory neurons supports the theory that the sense of smell is a very ancient sense.

The smell nerve fibers are among the most delicate in the body, and their paths are very complex. They are linked to many parts of the brain, especially the evolutionarily older parts that make up what is called the limbic system. These parts of the brain are involved with emotions and sexual behavior. Some smell nerve fibers, for example, reach to the hypothalamus, a part of the brain that contains centers controlling appetite, fear, anger, and even pleasure. Other smell fibers go high up into the cerebral cortex (the "thinking" part of the brain), and still others loop down to the brain stem, where breathing and other automatic functions are controlled.

Scientists refer to the olfactory nerves and bulbs, their connections to various parts of the brain, and the limbic system as the smell brain or rhinencephalon (from Greek words meaning "nose in the head"). Researchers believe that these structures are the most primitive part of the brain. It corresponds to the original brain in our early ancestors, which was concerned mainly with smell functions. The other parts of the brain—for example, the cerebral cortex—are believed to have developed later in the course of evolution.

How Do You Smell?

Now you know the structures and path that take an odor from the nose to the brain, but very important questions still remain. How do the receptors in the nasal passage determine what messages to send, and how does the brain identify them as particular odors? Actually, scientists aren't exactly sure. Many theories have been suggested, but none of them has yet been firmly proven.

Odor particles stimulate a response in the receptor cells that is transmitted to the brain and interpreted as a specific smell. But just what is it about those particles that the receptor cells recognize? Is it their chemical composition? Is it their size and shape? Is it how fast they move through the mucus? Do things that smell similar share similar chemical or physical properties? Are the nose's receptors specifically designed to receive particles of a particular size or shape or chemical composition?

In the study of other senses, like sight and sound, it is easy to make exact measurements. The frequency of a sound determines how high or low it seems, while the length of light waves reflected from an object indicates its color. But there isn't any easy way to make this kind of measurement of smells.

In the 1930s, scientists studied the olfactory bulb's response to various smells. They discovered that different areas of the olfactory bulb appeared to be sensitive to different types of smells. Other researchers found that individual receptors in the olfactory bulb were sensitive to different odors. Researchers determined that we smell things by the messages the brain receives when different receptors are stimulated. When we smell a particular smell, such as an apple, some receptors are stimulated, others aren't, and the specific combination is like a code the brain interprets as an apple.

A theory that became popular in the 1960s focused on the molecular shape of odor particles. It was suggested that different classes of smells have similar molecular shapes. The body's smell receptors are designed to fit these various shapes. If an odor molecule stimulates only one type of receptor, then we smell only that smell; but if other receptors are stimulated as well, there is a blend of odors. Dr. John Amoore, of the U.S. De-

Dr. John Amoore classified odors according to the characteristic shapes of their molecules. Each molecule fits into a suitably shaped receptor protein.

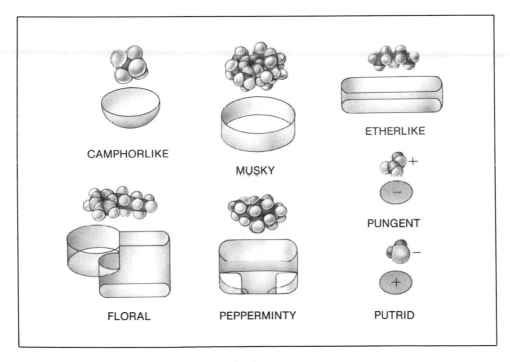

partment of Agriculture, proposed that there are five primary classes of odors, or primary smells, which have specific molecular shapes. They include (1) camphorlike (spherical-shaped); (2) musky (disk-shaped); (3) floral (kite-shaped—disk-shaped with a flexible tail); (4) pepperminty (wedge-shaped); and (5) etherlike (rod-shaped). In addition, Dr. Amoore suggested two other categories: (6) pungent and (7) putrid, which were classes of odors that were based not on their shape but on the electric charge of their particles.

Dr. Amoore's theory seemed to work in many situations. Researchers were able to alter molecular shapes, and the result indeed "smelled" the way the theory predicted. However, later studies by Dr. Amoore and other researchers determined that there probably are many more "primary" smells involved—at least thirty of them.

In 1991 Drs. Richard Axel and Linda Buck of Columbia University reported that they had isolated a family of smell genes from the nasal lining of rats. Each of these genes carries the blueprints for a particular odor receptor protein. The Columbia researchers found several hundred of these genes and believe there may be as many as a thousand of them—all active only in the nose and nowhere else in the body. Each receptor protein has a characteristic shape, and suitably shaped odor molecules fit into it. A particular odor molecule would stimulate a combination of different receptors. Various combinations of the thousand receptors could thus identify an almost unlimited number of different smells—more than enough to account for the ten thousand odors that humans can smell and the even greater variety that other animals can pick up.

The family of smell receptors is considerably more complicated than the receptors for color vision. All the thousands of colors we can distinguish are recognized with only three types of receptors: for red, green, and blue light. The fine differences that permit us to tell a bright grass green from chartreuse, for example, are the result of complicated processing of information in the brain. Odor information, on the other hand, is "preprocessed" by the many kinds of receptors in the nose, and not as much brain work is needed.

Recent experiments on rats have produced another result that may apply to humans, as well. A team headed by brain researcher Solomon Snyder of Johns Hopkins University in Baltimore discovered that a tiny duct at the tip of the rat's nose continually sprays a fine mist into the inhaled air. The mist contains proteins

Odorant-binding proteins collect and concentrate odor molecules from the air.

that bind to odor molecules. These odorant-binding proteins (OBPs) have cup-shaped openings into which the odor molecules fit. After picking them up, the proteins carry the odor molecules up through the mucus to the olfactory cells. The OBPs help to concentrate the odor molecules from the air, bringing similar ones together, which may explain how odor chemicals can be detected in such tiny amounts.

Different smells have different detection thresholds—that is, different numbers of particles need to be present before a person will notice the smell. Our sensitivity to smells may also be influenced by various factors, from the time of day to our emotional state. Under stress, a person tends to flare the nostrils and breathe more rapidly, bringing in more air; the blood supply to the olfactory areas increases, and the olfactory cells are also affected by stimulating messages from the nerves involved in getting the body ready to cope with an emergency. All these effects of stress combine to make us more sensitive to smells, lowering their detection thresholds.

On the other hand, sensitivity to smells is decreased when we are exposed to the same smell for a long time. We become adapted to the smell, by an effect called olfactory fatigue.

Olfactory Fatigue

Have you ever noticed that the delicious odors you smelled when you first walk into a bakery seem to fade away as you wait in line? Or perhaps you have visited a public rest room that hasn't been cleaned often enough. The smell seems disgusting at first, and you don't know how you will bear it, but by the time you leave you don't seem to be noticing the bad smell anymore.

These effects are examples of olfactory fatigue. When a smell particle reaches a receptor cell on the olfactory membrane, it fills up a spot. If the smell is strong, soon all the receptors that respond to that particular odor are filled. Those receptor cells have already sent their smell messages to the brain. They will not be able to fire again until the odor chemicals have been disposed of.

Olfactory fatigue may raise the detection thresholds not only for the particular smell that caused it but for other smells as well. When we become adapted to a smell, it can influence the quality of other odors, in addition to their apparent strength. If we breathe in a whiff of pine cleaner, for example, the smell of a chocolate cookie might not be as strong—or as good. That is the principle behind some "deodorizers." They do not really remove the odors in a room; instead, they send out an odor of their own that overwhelms the smell receptors, producing a sort of jamming effect. Some deodorizers have a general effect. Once they have flooded the olfactory receptors, we can't smell anything, not even pleasant smells. (Under the effect of this kind of room deodorant, you might not mind the smell of the cat's litter box anymore, but you won't enjoy the tempting smells of dinner cooking, either.) Recently, researchers have produced some more effective chemicals to block out bad odors. They seem to react with the specific olfactory receptors that respond to bad odors like rancid food or pet urine, while leaving the ability to smell pleasant odors unaffected.

Smell fatigue can sometimes be avoided by taking quick whiffs rather than smelling continuously. That is rather hard for humans to do—we smell automatically as we breathe. But rabbits, which depend much more on smell than we do, have a special device that permits them to smell more effectively. Flaps of skin open and close over the nostrils, much as our blinking eyelids continually cover and expose our eyes. Their action allows the rabbit to keep sniffing, bringing in new currents of air as its smell receptors recover from the last stimulation.

Smells and Memories

Many studies have shown that people remember smells more accurately than they do other sense impressions and retain the memories for longer periods of time. In one study, for example, volunteers were exposed to a series of new smells and taught to recognize them. Retests showed that they remembered the smells as well a month after they had first learned them as they did after a few minutes. In another study, people were found to recall up to 65 percent of the test smells a year after they were first presented. They recalled only 50 percent of a comparable series of photographs four months after the first viewing.

Not only are smells recalled very well, but smells tend to bring back vivid memories of people, places, and events with which they were linked in a person's past experience. The smell of fresh-baked cookies might bring back a scene in your grandmother's kitchen; the odor of a disinfectant might recall an unhappy visit to a hospital emergency room when you needed stitches for a bad cut.

The reason for the strong link between smell and memories is found in the way smell messages are sent into the brain. One main route of the olfactory neurons leads to the hippocampus, where long-term memories are formed. There are also links to other parts of the limbic system, which are involved in emotional

feelings. Strong emotions during an experience help to strengthen the memory of it. This link makes sense for an animal's survival: Smell messages are involved in some of the most important and basic parts of life, such as finding food, escaping from danger, and mating.

4

Smell Disorders

Compared to many members of the animal kingdom, we humans rank pretty low in smelling ability. A dog's sense of smell, remember, is a million times as keen as ours. And yet our ability to distinguish a wide range of different odors matches that of almost any other animal. In fact, our nose can identify thousands of odors—far more than any instrument ever invented.

Among individual humans, the variation in smelling ability is enormous. Researchers have found that people have different sensitivities to a particular odor. Some can detect a lower level than others. Eating asparagus, for example, gives urine a strong, distinctive odor, but only 10 percent of the public can pick up this odor in low concentrations. The vast majority of people do not detect it at all. Some people with otherwise normal smell abilities cannot smell the mercaptan odor of skunks. (A small percentage of the people who can smell it find skunk odor very pleasant.) According to smell researcher Chuck Wysocki, "Everybody has an odor blind spot. Nearly every person with a normal sense of smell has trouble smelling at least one basic odor that's obvious to other people." There is evidence that at least some of the individual differences in smell ability are hereditary.

The Great Smell Survey

Our understanding of individual differences in smelling abilities took a giant step forward in 1989, when *National Geographic* magazine announced the results of its giant smell survey. The September 1986 issue had included scratch-and-sniff strips containing six different odor chemicals, enclosed in tiny capsules that broke open to release the odor when the strip was scratched. The six test odors were selected to represent important types of smells:

- androstenone, a human body odor, found in sweat
- isoamyl acetate, the scent of bananas and pears, representing the group of food-related odors
- galaxolide, a synthetic musk, similar to an animal scent and used in perfumes
- eugenol, the odor of cloves, representing familiar spicy smells
- mercaptans, a mixture of sulfur compounds with a foul odor
- rose, to represent sweet, pleasant floral odors

Readers were asked to smell each odor and try to identify it. They also filled out a questionnaire indicating their sex, age, race, allergies, illnesses, and other facts about themselves. More than 1.5 million people responded to the magazine survey. Their

The National Geographic *survey asked readers to try to identify six different odors enclosed in scratch-and-sniff strips.*

replies revealed a great deal about human smelling abilities.

For instance, women can smell better than men. This was found to be true at all ages: five-year-old girls, for instance, outscored five-year-old boys. The ability to smell diminishes with age. Smokers do not smell as well as nonsmokers. Two out of every three people have temporarily lost their sense of smell because of a cold, allergy, accident, or some other cause. (In such cases the sense of taste is also dulled because much of what we perceive as taste is actually the odor of the food.) And most surprising, if the people who responded to the survey are a representative sample of the total population, more than two million Americans cannot smell at all!

Smell Defects

The two million Americans who have lost their sense of smell completely suffer from a problem that doctors call *anosmia*. For an additional eight million Americans, the ability to detect odors is reduced, far below normal levels. These people suffer from *hyposmia*.

Some people smell things "the wrong way"—for instance, the ones who think skunk odors are great. People with that kind of problem do not usually complain, but doctors see a lot of patients with the opposite defect: They are bothered by persistent unpleasant odors that no one else seems able to detect. They find normally pleasant odors, like that of a rose, unbearably obnoxious. Louis XI, who ruled France in the fifteenth century, was known as "the terrible king." His attitude problems were probably the result of a smell disorder: It is said that he thought everything around him stank terribly.

Sometimes during pregnancy a woman finds that her ability to smell goes haywire. Things that used to smell good don't anymore. Doctors are not sure why this happens. Some think it may be due to the extra hormones in the mother-to-be's blood. Epilepsy is another condition that can do strange things to a person's sense of smell. For a few days before a seizure, some epileptics find that familiar things don't smell the way they usually do. In some cases of epilepsy, a strong odor abruptly ends a seizure. Scientists are still speculating about why these things happen.

People who lose their sense of smell lose more than the ability to enjoy the many pleasant smells in the world around them. They lose an early-warning device that could alert them to escaping gas or spoiled food. A loss of smell also means a great reduction of the ability to taste foods. People suffering from anosmia or hyposmia often lose their appetite and their enjoyment of food; they tend to neglect good eating habits and may end up suffering from malnutrition. Many people who suffer from smell disorders become depressed. They lose their capacity to enjoy many of life's pleasures.

Anosmia can have many different causes. Some people are born with the disorder and never know what it's like to smell. The cause may be a hereditary lack of some important enzyme. But most people develop anosmia because of an accident or illness, or due to the aging process.

Head injuries have resulted in temporary or even permanent loss of smell for thousands of people. An infection in the upper respiratory tract may temporarily block the nasal passages and interfere with smell. (Do you remember your last cold, when your nose was all stuffed up? What did your supper taste like? Not much.) Allergies also block the nasal passages and can produce temporary losses of smell ability. Polyps, or growths, in the nasal or sinus cavities can lead to hyposmia or even anosmia. Hormonal problems have led to smell problems in some cases. Illnesses such as Alzheimer's disease, Parkinson's disease, Huntington's disease, and others often result in hyposmia or anosmia. In rare cases the cause of smell difficulties is a brain tumor. Usually, though, the cause is less drastic. Even cavities in the teeth can result in difficulty with smelling.

The mental illness schizophrenia is often accompanied by many strange smell effects. Patients often have an unusually keen sense of smell, and they may smell common odors abnormally, thinking that pleasant odors smell bad. Sometimes they have "smell hallucinations," smelling things that aren't there.

Sometimes medical treatments for an ailment can result in a loss of smell sensitivity. Some people who have cancer and undergo radiation treatment in the head and neck regions report that they can't smell as well as they used to. Medications and insecticides can interfere with the ability to smell. Usually, when the medication or exposure to insecticide is stopped, normal smell returns.

In many cases, a reduction or loss of the ability to smell is a result of aging. It is estimated that more than half of all people over sixty-five have serious hyposmia, with many suffering from a total loss of smell.

Diagnosing and Treating Smell Disorders

Finding out if a person has a smell disorder is not as easy as diagnosing many other ailments. For instance, an eye chart and other standard tests can quickly tell if a person has a vision problem. With smell, it's not so simple. In fact, researchers and their colleagues often disagree on whether a particular patient really has a smell problem at all.

There are more than seven hundred clinics in the United States that test for and treat smell disorders. They use several main types of diagnostic tests.

After asking questions about the problem, the doctor may ask the patient to identify a certain odor. To do this the doctor uses a device called an olfactometer, which enables patients to sniff a measurable amount of an odor through a nozzle hooked up to the machine. The doctor starts with a very small amount of the test odor and then gradually increases it until the patient is able to detect it. The doctor may ask the patient to compare different smells, and tell how their odor changes with different concentrations of each.

Smell disorders can be diagnosed with an olfactometer (left) *or with scratch-and-sniff tests* (right).

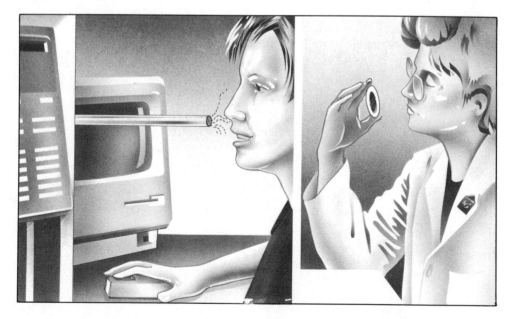

Scratch-and-sniff tests are now the most popular. The person scratches a treated patch on the paper to release the scent and then tells what, if anything, he or she smells. Dr. Richard Doty, director of the Clinical Smell and Taste Research Center at the University of Pennsylvania Hospital, has developed a scratch-and-sniff test to distinguish among fifty common odors, including bubble gum, licorice, gasoline, and pizza.

Can a person with a smell disorder recover and regain a normal sense of smell? That depends on the problem. If a specific chemical or medication is causing the disorder, then removing the culprit will usually lead to full recovery. In the case of a respiratory infection, when the cold or flu or sinus problem clears up, normal smell returns. In the case of seasonal allergies, relief comes when the irritating plant stops producing pollen; meanwhile antihistamines or injections to reduce the patient's sensitivity may ease the difficulties. If polyps are blocking the nasal passages, removing them will allow air to reach the smell receptors and solve the problem. In the case of a brain tumor, an operation may be the solution. Fortunately, for most people who are young and healthy, smell problems are only temporary.

5

Smell Signatures

A few years ago, the New York City Police Department conducted an experiment. A police detective started out in Central Park, cut across an area where a rock concert attended by fifty-five thousand people had been held the night before, passed through a meadow where nine softball games were going on, detoured onto a roadway where dozens of people from nearby apartments were walking their dogs, and hid in some bushes. Then a trained bloodhound was given the policeman's jacket to sniff. The dog started off confidently, following the invisible trail—and found the hidden policeman within five minutes!

The scent the bloodhound followed was produced by sweat chemicals and microscopic bits of dead skin that had flaked off with each step the policeman took. The dog was able to keep on the trail because each person has a highly individual smell—as unique as a signature or a fingerprint. Even the confusing odors from the people playing softball and walking dogs (as well as the traces left by the thousands at the concert the night before) did not confuse the keen-nosed bloodhound.

Personal Smell

A person's individual smell signature is produced by a number of sources. The air breathed out may contain various odor-producing chemicals. Perhaps there is a whiff of onion from the hamburger you had for lunch; or if you haven't been brushing and flossing regularly, your breath may carry a hint of decay from the food particles caught between your teeth. Odors from the environment, such as cigarette smoke, the hot oils from a fast-food kitchen, or the scents of soaps, lotions, and perfumes, may cling to a person's skin and clothing.

The skin itself is probably the largest source of personal odor, though. Tiny glands open onto the skin surface through narrow holes called pores. Some of these are oil glands at the base of hairs. The oils they produce help to keep the hair and skin smooth, but they also contribute to a person's characteristic smell. Even "smellier" are the products of a type of sweat gland called the apocrine gland. These glands are also found in hairy parts of the body, especially in the armpits and the genital regions. (The apocrine sweat glands become active at puberty, when coarse hair grows in these areas.) The watery sweat that pours off your face and body when you are hot or exercising heavily is produced by a different kind of sweat gland (the eccrine sweat gland); eccrine sweat is mainly salty water and has very

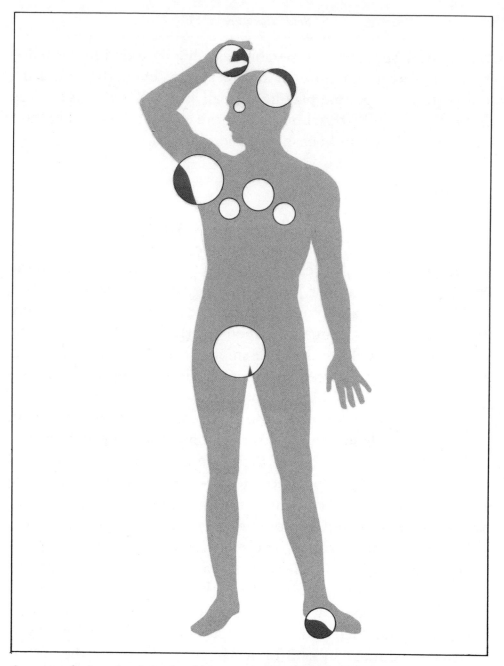

Scent-producing glands in the skin are concentrated in certain key areas of the body.

little odor. But apocrine sweat is thicker—a sticky white, gray, or yellowish fluid, with large amounts of complex chemicals.

Like the eccrine sweat glands, the apocrine glands respond to high temperatures, but they are also strongly stimulated by emotions—when you are nervous or frightened, for example. A person also tends to sweat more under the arm that is used more—if you are righthanded, your right armpit will tend to smell more than your left. And studies have shown that there are sex differences in the apocrine smells. (Males are smellier than females.)

The chemicals in apocrine sweat have odors of their own. However, the smell mixture is made much richer and stronger by the action of bacteria, feeding on the sweat chemicals and bits of dead skin cells. The skin bacteria change some of the chemicals in apocrine sweat to stronger-smelling products. The body hairs help to hold moisture and provide support and shelter for hordes of these tiny microbes. (A single square centimeter of skin in the armpit or on the scalp may be the home of millions of microscopic bacteria.) Even careful washing removes only a small fraction of the skin bacteria—and that is fortunate. These microbes are not disease bacteria; in fact, they may produce antibioticlike substances that can help to protect us from disease germs. The kinds of bacteria that make up this population of "microflora" vary from one person to another and from one part of the body to another.

Although the human sense of smell is not as keen as a dog's, we are able to recognize many of the fine differences that make up people's individual smell signatures. Helen Keller, who became blind and deaf at an early age, developed her sense of smell to an acute degree. She could recognize friends and visitors by the way they smelled, and she amazed them by greeting them by name. She said that just by smelling people she could tell the kind of work they did, from the telltale odors of wood, iron, paint, or drugs that clung to their skin and clothes. She could also tell—just by smell—if a person had come from the kitchen, the garden, or the sickroom.

The average person relies more on sight and sounds for information about the world and is rarely conscious of individual smells (unless they are unusually strong or "different"). And yet studies have shown that people are surprisingly good at identifying personal odors. In a series of tests, most of a group of mothers who had recently given birth were able to pick out an undershirt worn by their own baby from shirts worn by other infants in the nursery. Some of the mothers commented that the

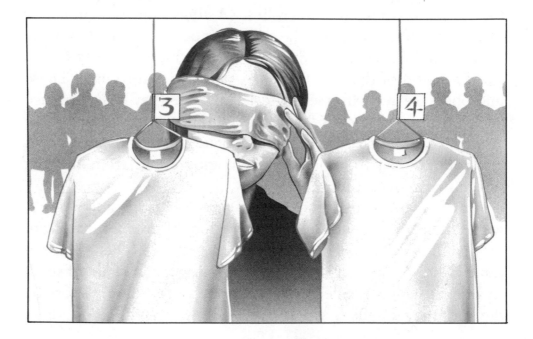

shirts smelled like other children in the family. (Interestingly, studies have also shown that breastfed human infants learn to recognize their mother's smell.) In another study, seventeen out of eighteen mothers with children from two to seven years of age were able to pick out their own child's T-shirt from shirts worn by other children. Sixteen of the mothers were also able to tell the difference between T-shirts worn by two of their own children.

Family Smells and Racial Differences

Is there some sort of "family smell"? These and other studies suggest that there is. Another group of fifteen mothers, with their three- to eight-year-old children, were given T-shirts to wear for three nights in a row. Then a group of people were given the shirts to smell and asked to match up the mothers with their children. The groups' scores were much better than those that would have been expected by mere guessing. But in a similar experiment matching T-shirts worn by husbands and wives, the shirt sniffers were not able to score as many correct matches. Such studies suggest that heredity plays a larger role than environment in determining people's individual smells.

These findings agree with observations that people of different races have different characteristic smells. Some of these differences are due to variations in diet: People in India, for example, eat a lot of curry and spices, which is reflected in their body odor. Racial differences also depend to a large degree on hereditary traits. Orientals have very little body hair and few apocrine sweat glands. Koreans have little body odor even if they did not wash regularly; underarm odor is so rare among Japanese that they consider it an illness. Caucasians, on the other hand, have more body hair and apocrine glands. Blacks have even more of the glands. Such subtle smell differences can have an unconscious effect on people's attitudes and can contribute to misunderstanding and bad feelings among people of different races.

Personal Smell Recognition

A kitten is born with its eyes sealed shut, yet it is able to find its way to its mother's teats when she lies down to suckle her litter. In fact, each kitten in the litter soon settles down to its own personal nipple on its mother's belly. Researchers have

Suckling kittens find their milk supply by smell. Each recognizes its own nipple on its mother's belly.

Dogs identify each other by checking characteristic body smells.

discovered that the kitten finds its way to the milk supply and recognizes its assigned nipple by smell.

Mammal mothers and babies of many species use their sense of smell to recognize each other. Fur seals give birth on island beaches after a long ocean migration, and then they must go down to the water periodically to get food. The individual smell helps to guide them back to their own pup on the crowded beaches.

In most mammal species, a mother will not feed another mother's infant, even if it is the same age as her own. But she may be persuaded to accept an orphan if it is smeared with her own scent or that of her own young. Sheep raisers use that trick to get ewes to raise orphaned lambs.

Although humans do not usually use personal smell recognition consciously, most other mammals rely on their noses as the most dependable guide to identifying individuals. When two dogs meet, their greeting takes the form of sniffing—usually at the tail end, where the personal smells are the strongest. Cats, mice, horses—practically all mammals—automatically check the smell signatures of any individuals of their species that they meet, whether they are strangers or the closest family members. (Some scientists believe that the human practice of kissing developed from the same kind of "smell ID check.")

The variety of odors that make up the personal smell contains a wealth of information: not only an identification as unique as a fingerprint but also an indication of the individual's sex, age, and even mood. In fact, for most animals with a good sense of smell, odors make up a language that can be used for communicating with others of their species.

6

Communicating by Smell

An ant's eyesight is not very good, but it has a keen sense of smell—keen enough to sniff out a crumb of food on the ground nearby. Tapping and probing the morsel with its feelers, it gets an idea of its shape and size, then picks it up and carries it back to the ant nest. An ant can carry objects much larger than its own weight; but what if the food it has found is too large for it to carry—a dead beetle, perhaps, or a piece of jelly doughnut that someone dropped? Hurrying back to the nest, the ant pauses from time to time to touch the tip of its abdomen to the ground. Each time, it releases a tiny drop of chemical through its stinger. Back at the nest, the ant is met by others from the colony. Sniffing at the ant with their antennas, they soon show signs of excitement. Some start busily repairing the nest; others go off to care

Ants use pheromones to lay down odor trails that nestmates can follow to a food source.

for the young ants; and some rush outside, sniffing at the ground. Soon they pick up the traces of scent the returning ant had laid down. Before long, there is a line of ants, moving out from the nest along the odor trail to the food. When they reach it, they work together to chop it into smaller pieces and carry the pieces back to the nest.

Smell Talk

Not only ants but practically all animals that have a good sense of smell use odors as a kind of language. Different smell chemicals and combinations of them can carry a lot of information. They can provide a complete personal identification and also communicate moods and feelings like contentment or fear. Some animals transfer their personal smells to objects around them—like an identification label ("This rock belongs to A. Rabbit") or a chemical *No Trespassing* sign. Odors make convenient trail markers, and they can also serve as a means of advertising. Female cats and some other mammals, for example, announce their readiness to mate using scent signals.

Chemicals that an animal produces and releases into its surroundings to communicate with others of its species are called *pheromones*. (*Phero-* comes from a Greek word meaning "to carry"; the ending, *-mones,* emphasizes their similarity to hormones, which are chemicals used for communication inside the body.) Some animals also produce smells to communicate with animals of other species; these are called *allomones*. (The prefix comes from a word meaning "other.") The best known allomone is the spray that a frightened skunk squirts out from special scent glands on its rear. Skunk spray contains mercaptans, sulfur compounds that are particularly strong and unpleasant-smelling. If a skunk is attacked, it douses the attacker with this smell and then may take advantage of the shock and confusion to escape. A meeting with a skunk serves as a learning experience—few animals would care to get sprayed again, so they quickly learn to leave skunks alone. And, because smelly sulfur compounds are often produced by bacteria in rotting foods, the odor also identifies the skunk with something that is not good to eat.

Poisonous plants and insects are often brightly colored or marked with easy-to-recognize patterns. Animals quickly learn that species with such patterns are not good to eat. Many of these plants and insects also produce smell warnings, which scientists have discovered contain compounds from the chemical group of pyrazines. Tiger moths, monarch butterflies, and ladybugs all advertise their poisonous nature with brightly colored markings and pyrazine smells. One researcher suggests that pyrazines work so well as an alarm smell because these chemicals are produced in the smoke of forest and prairie fires and can thus serve as an easily recognized, planetwide danger signal.

The monarch butterfly, ladybug, and tiger moth all produce pyrazine smells to warn predators that they are not good to eat.

Insect Scent Messages

Ants are social insects; they live and work together in large communities. They need to be able to communicate with others in the group to coordinate their activities, and pheromones provide them with a useful and important language. Odor trails help ants to locate food and bring it back to the anthill. The amounts of the odor chemicals are amazingly small. A biologist at Harvard University calculated, for example, that one milligram (about the same weight as a grain of salt) of the trail pheromone of the leaf-cutter ant would be enough to lead a column of ants around the world three times! The ants from the nest can not only pick up the trail, but they can tell which way it is pointing. (If an ant crosses a sheet of paper while laying down its odor trail, and then the paper is turned around 180°, the ants from the nest become confused when they reach the paper—the trail is pointing the wrong way. After milling around for a bit, though, they pick up the trail and continue on to the food.) The odor trail also holds some more information: If the food source is a large one, the ants that return with pieces of it lay down more pheromone marks, and the scent gets stronger. This tells the ants at the nest that there is more work to be done.

Ants also use smells to identify members of their own community. If an ant from another nest tries to enter the anthill, the ant does not smell right to the guards at the entrance, and they attack it. However, when researchers dab a bit of scent from the nest on the "foreign" ants, then they are allowed to enter. The same kind of thing happens naturally, too. Various kinds of beetles make a pheromone that mimics the ant scent. Not only are they allowed to enter the anthill and share the ants' shelter, but the ants even feed them. With their counterfeit chemicals, the beetles are mistaken for helpless baby ants.

Other ant pheromones act as danger signals. An ant produces them when it is attacked or hurt. The other ants in the area smell the alarm chemicals and immediately get ready to fight or run away. There are even "death pheromones," which form when dead ants decay. Worker ants who smell these chemicals pick up the dead ant and carry it out of the nest to the refuse heap. Researchers have dabbed the death pheromones on the body of a living ant. As soon as the ant returns to the nest, its nestmates immediately pick it up and carry it out. No matter how it kicks and squirms, they seem convinced it is dead, and they carry it out to the dump again each time it tries to return to the anthill.

Other insects also rely heavily on smell communication. When a bee stings, for example, it releases an alarm pheromone that prompts other bees in the neighborhood to attack as well. (The Africanized honeybees, descended from bees introduced to the Western Hemisphere from Africa, have earned the nickname of "killer bees" because they are so aggressive. They make a very strong alarm pheromone, which causes them to sting in large numbers with very little provocation.) The honeybee queen produces a special pheromone that keeps the worker bees from laying eggs. During her mating flight, the queen's pheromone attracts the drones that fly after her. Pheromones are also important in a termite nest, helping to identify the members of the group and to determine which termites will perform all the necessary jobs.

Social insects like bees, wasps, ants, and termites have to coordinate many activities and use a complex assortment of pheromones to communicate—almost a sort of "smell language." The need for communication is not as great for insects that do not live in groups, but many of them use their sense of smell to find food, and many use pheromones to find a mate.

Moths, for example, may spread out over great distances to feed. How can a female moth find males of her species when she is ready to mate? She does it by producing a sex pheromone that helps the males to find her. The volatile chemical spreads through the air and is carried by the winds far and wide. Each tiny hair in the male moth's feathery antenna contains special sense cells that react to particular odors. Male silkworm moths, for example, respond to a chemical called bombykol, which is produced in the abdomen of female silkworm moths. A single molecule of bombykol in the air is enough to start a male silk-

The male silkworm moth can follow a sex attractant odor for miles to find a mate.

worm moth flying upwind, searching for more of the odor. As he gets closer to the female that released the sex pheromone, its concentration in the air increases. On he flies, until he finds his mate. (Actually he may also find some competition. Each female produces only about ten-millionths of a milligram of bombykol, but this tiny amount would be enough to attract one billion males!)

Not all moths have such a simple sex attractant. Female oriental fruit moths, for example, release a sex pheromone containing three different chemicals, mixed in definite amounts. When scientists tried to produce synthetic sex attractants for this kind of moth, they found that the males would respond only if the scientists included all three chemicals and got the blend exactly right.

The first male that reaches the female sends out a scent of his own, rather similar to the female's pheromone. This confuses male moths that arrive later, and they lose precious time while the winner of the race is claiming his prize. The males of some moth species also produce sex pheromones of their own. These scent chemicals act as recognition signals, reassuring the female that the male is of the right species. Scientists have found that moth species which live in the same area as other, closely related species are most likely to use this way of identifying the most suitable mates.

Researchers have isolated the chemicals in sex attractants from various insect pests, such as gypsy moths, pink bollworms, and cockroaches. They have developed methods of synthesizing the pheromones artifically and have been testing them as lures for trapping and killing the pests.

Insects rely heavily on instincts in their responses to life's challenges. A male silkworm moth that detects bombykol, for example, immediately begins to fan his wings and then takes off into the air. (In one experiment, marked male moths were released a mile away from females and returned within about ten minutes.) Ants that smell the death pheromone on one of their nestmates will carry it out of the anthill, even if it is struggling violently and is very much alive. Mammals—from mice to donkeys—also use pheromones to communicate with others of their species. However, their reactions to them are much more complex and are influenced by their experiences.

Trails, Territories, and Signals

When you take a dog for a walk, resign yourself to competing for its attention with dozens of fascinating distractions. The dog continually leans down to sniff at the ground; if allowed, it will scamper off to follow intriguing trails that are invisible to you.

The dog's actions may seem purposeless, but it is actually gathering information about the neighborhood creatures and their recent activities. Lingering smells inform it that a cat passed by or a squirrel scampered up a tree. Most interesting (to the dog) is the smell news about the other dogs in the area. Each one has left pheromone traces with every step, from scent glands on its paws. Other glands next to the anus put scent markers on dogs' feces, and still other glands pour pheromones into their urine. Your dog, reading these odor traces, can tell exactly which dogs have passed by recently, their sex, age, and even their mood. (The "scent of fear" can warn dogs of possible trouble ahead.) Meanwhile, your dog is leaving its own contributions to the neighborhood "smell newsletter" when it squats to deposit a pile of feces, or pauses to squirt urine on a tree trunk, fire hydrant, or some other object.

Many mammals use pheromones to mark trails or outline the boundaries of their home territory. Male cats "spray" a mixture of urine and scent chemicals on trees, bushes, and rocks to inform other cats of their presence. Cats also have scent glands on their cheeks and chin; they mark familiar objects (such as their human owners) by rubbing their faces against them. Lions and other wild cat relatives use scent markings in similar ways.

Wolves, foxes, and other dog relatives mark their trails and territories in much the same way as domestic dogs. Members of a wolf pack mark their trails with urine and feces, but "lone

Animals like the white-tailed deer (left) *and domestic cat* (right) *use pheromones produced in scent glands to mark their territories.*

wolves" try to avoid attracting attention to themselves and move off the trail to deposit their feces in the underbrush. Bears urinate on the ground, then roll in their urine and rub their wet fur against trees to leave scent marks. Bears from other areas usually will not enter a territory whose boundaries have been marked in this way.

Not only the hunters of the animal world but also many prey animals will mark and defend territories against others of their own kind. Bristlelike hairs on the legs of white-tailed deer help to spread the scent from the tarsal glands located there. Some antelopes use scent glands around their eyes to mark grass stalks; others smear the oils from these glands on their bodies to help spread the scent. Rabbits mark the boundaries of their territories with scent glands under the chin.

Among the mammals, smell also plays a very important part in finding and recognizing a mate. In most species, the female is able to mate only for brief periods of time. In some species, this receptive period occurs only once or twice a year; in others the sexual cycle repeats every few days. For a species to survive, there must be effective ways to bring males and females together during this brief time when young can be produced. Generally, the female announces her receptive state to the males in the area with pheromones. The male also has his own sex pheromones, which may help to make females receptive or to influence their choice of a mate.

Researchers believe that humans, like other mammals, produce body scents that could act as pheromones. But we humans rely less on our sense of smell than most other mammals do. Moreover, our behavior is determined less by automatic, instinctive reactions and more by what we have learned from personal experiences and cultural customs. Some pheromonelike chemicals have been isolated from human sweat, but they often do not produce the reactions that might be expected. For example, most people think that androstenol and androstenone, sweat chemicals that act as sex signals in other mammals, smell rather unpleasant.

Perhaps our reactions to human pheromones depend on the circumstances, or our reactions to natural body smells may no longer be "natural." As you'll see in the next chapter, people today—at least, in the United States—don't seem to like their human body smells very much.

7

Those Embarrassing Body Odors

Very young children find most odors pleasant. But it doesn't take long to learn that our culture considers certain odors offensive. By kindergarten, the average child already knows that "You stink!" is the ultimate insult.

The line between a normal personal smell and an offensive body odor seems like a very fine one these days. Among the odors considered objectionable are mainly those linked with "bathroom functions" and those associated with dirt and disease. So TV and radio commercials sell medicated soaps, mouthwashes, hair shampoos, underarm deodorants, and foot sprays that are guaranteed to kill germs and keep you smelling fresh. People shave their underarms to remove the hair that harbors smell-producing bacteria.

People didn't always have our present attitude toward body smells. In the Middle Ages, a "love apple" was a prized gift from a lady to her beau. She prepared it by peeling an apple, then placing it in her armpit until it had soaked up enough of her sweat to give her lover an aromatic remembrance of her. A few centuries later, the French emperor Napoleon wrote from the battlefront to his wife, Josephine: *Ne te lave pas; je reviens* ("Don't wash—I'm coming home"). In eighteenth-century England, though, people were not as enthusiastic about natural body odors. The famous writer Samuel Johnson was riding in a coach one day with a woman who remarked, "Sir, you smell!" Johnson was writing a dictionary, and he was far more careful about using words than he was about washing. "Madam, you are wrong," he corrected her. "You smell; I stink."

The skin smells that contribute to body odor are concentrated mainly in the areas that are heavily supplied with apocrine sweat glands, especially the armpits and the genital area. Underarm odor is not usually obvious unless the arm is raised. Biologists point out that armpits are a very convenient location for a rich source of pheromones, permitting the smell to be let out when desired in much the same way that a deer raises its flaplike tail to expose its anal scent glands.

The feet are another especially smelly part of the body. The sweat glands on the feet are very responsive to both temperature and emotions. They pour out sweat when we are "hot and bothered," and the constant pressure and friction of walking rubs off dead skin cells that help to feed the bacteria living on the skin. The spaces between the toes tend to remain warm and moist, especially when we wear shoes, providing a perfect breeding ground for bacteria. Researchers have found that some foot odor

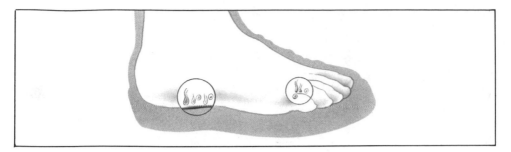

Bacteria feeding on dead skin cells moistened by sweat produce the typical "cheesy" foot odor.

is produced by a microbe used in making cheeses. Foot odor is so strong that it can soak into leather shoes; a dog can follow a trail of odor prints left by someone who walked by two weeks before. Some people's feet sweat (and smell) more than others. Bathing the feet with alcohol, using antiperspirants, or taking oral medications prescribed by a doctor can help someone bothered by sweaty feet.

Because the smell receptors in the nose adapt quickly to constantly present odors, people are not usually conscious of their own body odors, even when others might consider them particularly foul. When you sniff your underarm to determine whether you are socially acceptable or need to wash, you are able to pick up any sweaty scent because the armpit area is normally covered. Exposing it gives you a blast of more concentrated odor, to which your smell receptors have not yet had a chance to adapt.

Halitosis

Concern about bad breath is nothing new. The ancient Roman playwright Plautus commented, "My wife's breath smells awful. I would rather kiss a toad." In tenth-century Wales, bad breath was one of the few recognized grounds for divorce. Today people find bad breath so embarrassing that even close friends may be reluctant to tell you about it; and you will probably be annoyed or angry if someone does mention it "for your own good." Yet nearly everyone suffers from halitosis (bad breath) occasionally. Normal breath itself is composed of odorless gases, such as nitrogen, oxygen, carbon dioxide, and water vapors; the saliva produced in the mouth is also odorless. But odors can be added to the breath from sources in the mouth, as well as the lungs and sometimes the stomach.

Insufficient tooth brushing and flossing can leave food particles on the teeth. The mixture of food and saliva provides nourishment for mouth bacteria, which produce smelly by-products during their fermenting process. The odor is usually strongest just after awakening ("morning mouth"). This is because, during sleep, there is a reduced flow of saliva, and what is produced tends to lie in pools in the mouth rather than swishing around to provide a washing action as it does when you are awake. Tooth decay and gum disease contribute to the odor problem by adding foul-smelling hydrogen sulfide to the breath and also by producing pockets in which food particles can be trapped. Antihistamines and other medications may reduce the flow of saliva, producing a dry mouth and gum problems that can result in mouth odor. Drinking alcoholic beverages contributes the odor of alcohol and its chemical breakdown products to the breath and promotes the growth of odor-producing microbes in the mouth. Smoking contributes to halitosis in several ways: Smoke particles and tars deposited in the lungs may be exhaled, and smoking also decreases the flow of saliva and promotes the formation of hairlike growths on the tongue, which trap food particles.

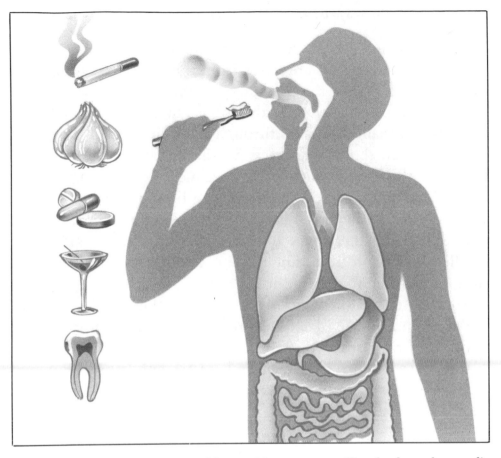

Bad breath may be caused by smoking, and by strong-smelling foods, such as garlic, certain drugs, alcoholic beverages, and tooth decay.

Mouthwashes that kill germs can help a bit with halitosis that is due to problems in the mouth (but probably not as much as brushing the teeth and flossing), but mainly they just cover up the unpleasant odors. That is all they do in the case of odors coming from the lungs or stomach. Such odors may be produced by various illnesses and also by eating strong-smelling foods like garlic. It is easy to imagine how a belch could send a blast of garlic breath up from the stomach; but how does the garlic smell get into the lungs? It is absorbed from the digestive system into the bloodstream, and the blood carries the odor chemicals to all parts of the body, including the lungs. In the lungs there is a continual exchange of gases through the thin walls of the blood capillaries and the tiny air sacs. So the garlic smell passes into the air in the lungs, which is then exhaled. In one experiment, doctors rubbed garlic on the soles of a boy's feet, then put his shoes back on and took him to a room in another part of the building where there was no trace of garlic in the air. They smelled his breath from time to time, and after about one hour, sure enough—the garlic odor appeared.

We tend to be unconscious of our own bad breath because we are constantly exposed to the smells from the mouth; but the odors due to gases expelled from the rectum (referred to as "flatus") are often a source of embarrassment, especially when their release is accompanied by rumblings, gurglings, or various explosive noises.

Flatus

A performer on the stage of the Moulin Rouge a century ago entertained his Paris audiences with "concerts" consisting of amazingly controlled passages of intestinal gas. It is said that his flatus was nearly odorless, although it was quite noisy. Most people, however, find the odor of the gas expelled from the rectum distressingly foul smelling.

Researchers have discovered that about 30 to 50 percent of intestinal gas is produced by bacterial fermentation of undigested food materials. The rest of the volume is made up of swallowed air. The bulk of the intestinal gases—nitrogen, oxygen, hydrogen, carbon dioxide, and methane—are odorless. Odor is contributed by such bacterial products as ammonia, hydrogen sulfide, fatty acids, and amines. Together they account for about 1 percent of the gas volume.

Emotional stress causes people to swallow air; carbonated soft drinks can also contribute gas that finds its way to the intestines. Certain foods are noted for their gas-producing effects. These include broccoli, cabbage, cauliflower, brussels sprouts, turnips, cucumbers, radishes, onions, and beans.

Flatus may be controlled by eating yogurt or other sources of *Lactobacillus acidophilus,* a "friendly" bacterium that multiplies in the intestine and crowds out gas-producing microbes.

Smells of Sickness

Tupa Mbae, a native healer in Paraguay, had an amazing ability to diagnose people's illnesses by smelling their shirts or underwear. He even performed some long-distance diagnoses for people in the United States. Such feats may sound unbelievable to us today, and yet, at one time doctors routinely used their noses as a guide in diagnosing their patients' problems.

Various diseases produce characteristic body or breath odors. Chemicals called ketones, produced in a diabetic's body, for example, give the breath a fruity odor. Certain types of cancer have a foul odor. Children born with phenylketonuria, or PKU (a hereditary inability to use a common amino acid that, as a result, can lead to mental retardation unless they are fed a special diet), have a "mousy" smell. Another hereditary disorder was named maple-syrup urine disease because of the characteristic smell of the babies' urine. People with fish odor syndrome lack a key digestive enzyme that helps to digest chemicals in beans, eggs, fish, and liver. An ammonialike odor suggests to an alert physician that the patient may have a kidney problem; a musky odor can be an early warning of liver problems; a fecal odor indicates that something is blocking the bowels. People with diphtheria have a sickeningly sweet smell; measles produces an odor like freshly plucked feathers; plague victims smell like apples; typhoid fever patients have an odor like freshly baked bread; and yellow fever produces a "butcher shop" odor. Fictional detectives make use of a real-life smell clue when they deduce cyanide poisoning from the odor of bitter almonds. Arsenic poisoning gives the victim a garlic odor.

Researchers are trying to devise machines that would automatically analyze the odors from a person's breath and body and diagnose illnesses from the gases present. Breathalyzers are already being used to determine alcohol levels of drunken drivers.

The Breathalyzer detects alcohol in the breath, which is an indication of the amount of alcohol in the person's blood.

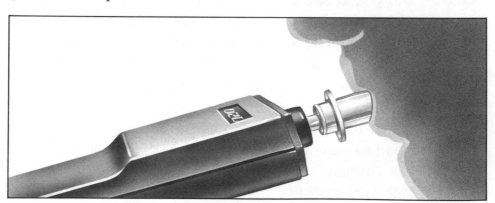

8

Frontiers of Smell Research

Many questions still remain unanswered on the subject of smell, our most ancient and subtle sense. In hundreds of laboratories around the world, scientists are searching for answers to some of them. The U.S. government is supporting much of this work, at universities and nonprofit health organizations, through the National Institute of Neurological and Communicative Disorders and Strokes (NINCDS). The food and perfume industries are also working actively on studies of smell in order to develop new aromas and fragrances.

One of the complications in smell research is the fact that most odors in nature are combinations of many different substances. Researchers have to sort out the various components of a "smell" in order to determine which ones are responsible for a particular effect.

Analyzing Smells

Two modern instruments have produced a revolution in smell research. In a gas chromatograph, the mixture of volatile chemicals that makes up a particular smell is carried by a flow of gas over a layer of absorbent material that holds some components more tightly than others. As the flow of "carrier gas" continues, the individual chemicals emerge from the chromatograph, one by one. Then these chemicals are sent into a mass spectrograph, which identifies them and gives important clues about their chemistry.

The gas chromatograph (left) and mass spectrograph (right) are used to analyze odor chemicals.

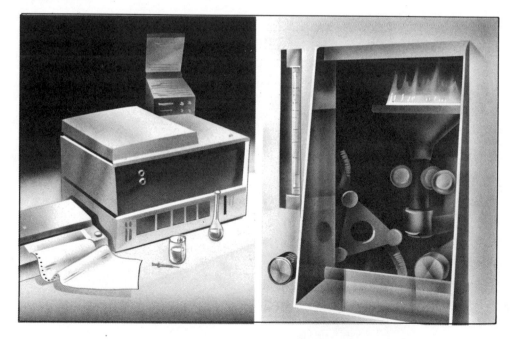

Using these instruments, researchers at Cornell University have developed a new technique of categorizing flavors (a mixture of taste and odor), which they call "charm odor analysis." Using gas chromatography, they separate different common foods such as margarine and butter, and end up with a wide range of different volatile substances. The machine does the separating, but the odors are detected by human volunteer sniffers. When the volunteer smells something coming out of the machine, he or she pushes a button. A computer records the results. The researcher dilutes the sample and tries the test again, continuing until the volunteer no longer smells anything. By screening the results, the researchers can usually tell which of the many components is really responsible for the particular odor of a food or common substance.

The Cornell lab is working on a number of practical problems. For instance, most people think that fresh orange juice has a better aroma than the packaged variety. The Cornell researchers discovered that the polyethylene used to line the package absorbs most of the main volatile chemical in orange juice, limonene. But their charm tests showed that the loss of limonene did not have much of an effect on the flavor. Studies are continuing to try to determine what other odor chemicals in orange juice are lost in processing.

Devising an Artificial Nose

Another problem in smell research is the fact that the sense of smell is so subjective. Different people respond to the same odor differently. An "artificial nose" could remove this confusing "human factor." A mechanical sniffer would also be free of the fatigue effect that quickly sets in when people continue to smell the same odor; a machine could go on smelling a particular odor indefinitely. So far, human noses are more sensitive than the best odor-detecting machines, but the gap is narrowing.

At Leeds University, in England, researchers have put together a "mechanical dog." This artificial sniffer takes up a whole room and consists of chromatographs, mass spectrographs, computers, and other devices. Even so, it is far less sensitive than the nose of a real dog. Using their mechanical dog, the researchers have examined the underarm sweat of human volunteers. They have already identified more than eighteen different volatile substances in underarm sweat.

The researchers at Leeds believe that by using all eighteen components of sweat, every single human being on earth could be "odor-printed"—with no two alike—just as fingerprints can tell any two humans apart. But to demonstrate how far we still have to go to duplicate living noses, the researchers regularly use real dogs to help in their investigations.

The Robotics Institute of Carnegie-Mellon University and Sandia National Laboratories are using semiconductor technology to develop artificial noses. They hope to use these devices in such wide-ranging areas as drug manufacture, food processing, and nuclear weapons safety procedures.

Learning About Smell Biology

At Duke University Medical School, physiologist Sidney Simon has developed an artificial nose using olfactory receptors—protein molecules found in the nasal passages that are sensitive to particular odors. In the nose, such receptors send a message to

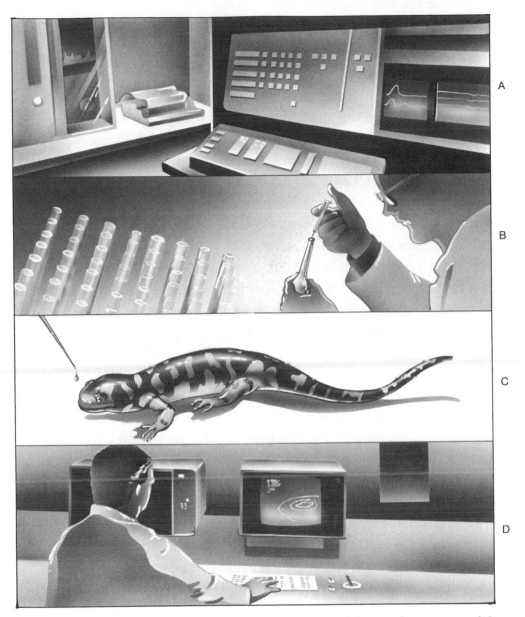

The "mechanical dog" (A) doesn't look much like a real dog, and current models can't smell as keenly as one. The study of smell receptors (B) and experiments on salamanders (C) are adding to our knowledge of smell. Neural net computer models (D) mimic the workings of the brain.

the brain when specific odor chemicals are present. By placing receptors in a test tube, Dr. Simon can study their action in ways that would be impossible in a human subject. His group has learned a great deal about how these receptors work.

Other researchers are also experimenting with living creatures. For instance, John Kauer and his team at the New England Medical Center in Boston are working with salamanders, studying the nerve cells in their olfactory bulb. With a special dye that changes color when the nerve cells are stimulated by a particular odor, researchers have discovered that neurons in the brain form a certain pattern when a particular odor chemical is smelled for the first time. Then, when it is smelled again, a different pattern is formed. Studying these patterns may provide clues as to how we learn to recognize and remember odors.

In other groups, researchers are using computers to simulate how the brain and olfactory nerves work during the smelling process. Gary Lynch, a neurobiologist, and Richard Granger, a computer scientist at the University of California, Irvine, have teamed up to design a computer model to predict how the rat smells odors. Their computer model uses a new form of computer technology known as neural nets. This copies how the brain distinguishes differences in the world about it. They have discovered, for instance, that the cells closest to the entrance of the nose of a rat tend to compare different odor molecules for similarities. Those farther in are more sensitive to the specific characteristics that distinguish one kind of odor chemical from another.

Many of the computer's predictions were later found to be true, when experiments were conducted on real rats in the laboratory.

Artificial Smells

Studies of fragrances and their effects on people are one of the most active areas of smell research today. This hot "new" field is also one of the oldest of human interests. The use of fragrance dates back at least six or seven thousand years, when Buddhists in China burned various plants during religious ceremonies and thus invented incense. At various times people have used extracts from flowers and spices and other aromatic substances such as animal musk as perfumes to make themselves more attractive. In the Middle Ages it was thought that pleasant smells could protect people from disease; actually, they only covered up the less pleasant smells of dirt and illness.

Today the biggest users of fragrances are the producers of foods and products like soap, shampoos, detergents, and toilet paper. (Even cat litter is made with an added fragrance—the scent of anise, which cats find attractive.) Fragrances are added to food products to help make up for the natural aromas lost during shipping and storage.

The supplies of natural fragrances would not be enough to satisfy all the needs of these industries—the manufacturer of one brand of soap uses more than two million pounds of fragrance each year! Researchers have analyzed the chemical makeup of various natural fragrances and produced artificial substitutes. For example, food researchers have isolated and synthesized the aromas of fresh-baked bread, corn chips, pizza, and chocolate. A synthetic fragrance added to one brand of detergent makes clothes smell sun-dried. One fragrance manufacturer has a library of one thousand compounds simulating the scents of foods, herbs, and rainy days.

The effects of smells on emotions, mood, and behavior are being studied actively. Researchers studying volunteers' brain-wave patterns have found that a spicy apple scent has a calming effect even greater than that of lavender, which had long been thought to be soothing. The smell of peppermint, on the other hand, is stimulating. British researchers have found a chemical in human armpit sweat, Osmone 1, that seems to have a tranquilizing effect, easing anxiety.

Much remains to be learned, but the results of such studies are already being applied. Scratch-and-sniff strips are widely used in ads, not only to sell perfume but also to trigger memories and associations—like the smell of leather upholstery attached to an ad for Rolls-Royce cars. Dispensers that spray the scent of chocolate around the candy shelves in a supermarket or a piña colada scent near a display of alcoholic beverages are designed to stimulate people's appetites and subtly persuade them to buy the products. The new specialty of aromatherapy combines the use of scented oils with relaxing massage. Mood-stimulating room scents are gaining in popularity, and there is even an "Aroma Disk Player" with choices of scents including "Movie Time" (hot buttered popcorn), "Country Roads," "Christmas Tree," "Fireplace," and "Baby Powder."

Smell research is still a rather new area. Much remains to be learned. But as more researchers enter the field, we are gaining fascinating new insights into this basic yet mysterious aspect of ourselves.

For Further Reading

The following books and articles, written for an adult audience, may be of interest to readers who wish to learn more about various aspects of smell.

Ackerman, Diane. *A Natural History of the Senses.* New York: Random House, 1990.

Blakeslee, Sandra. "Pinpointing the Pathway of Smell." *New York Times*, 4 October 1988, p. C1.

Brody, Robert. "The Sweet Sense of Smell." *American Health*, May 1986, pp. 55–59.

Burton, Maurice. *Animal Senses.* Princton: Van Nostrand, 1965.

Downer, John. *Supersense: Perception in the Animal World.* New York: Henry Holt, 1989.

Droscher, Vitus B. *The Magic of the Senses.* New York: Dutton, 1969.

Gibbons, Boyd. "The Intimate Sense of Smell." *National Geographic*, September 1986, pp. 324–361 (with Smell Survey).

Gilbert, Avery N., and Charles J. Wysocki. "The Smell Survey Results." *National Geographic*, October 1987, pp. 514–525.

McCutcheon, Marc. *The Compass in Your Nose*. Los Angeles: Tarcher, 1989.

MacDonald, David, and Richard Brown. "The Smell of Success." *New Scientist*, 23 May 1985, pp. 10–14.

Monmaney, Terence. "Are We Led by the Nose?" *Discover*, September 1987, pp. 48–56.

National Institute of Neurological and Communicative Disorders and Stroke. *Fact Sheet: Smell and Taste Disorders*. Bethesda, Md.: National Institutes of Health, 1985 (pamphlet).

Rivlin, Robert, and Karen Gravelle. *Deciphering the Senses*. New York: Simon & Schuster, 1984.

Smith, Jillyn. *Senses & Sensibilities*. New York: Wiley, 1989.

Sommerville, Barbara, David Gee, and June Averill. "On the Scent of Body Odour." *New Scientist*, 10 July 1986.

Sommerville, Barbara, and Michael Green. "The Sniffing Detective." *New Scientist*, 20 May 1989.

Whitfield, Philip, and D. M. Stoddart. *Hearing, Taste and Smell*. Tarrytown, N.Y.: Torstar Books, 1984.

Wilentz, Joan Steen. *The Senses of Man*. New York: Crowell, 1968.

Winter, Ruth. *The Smell Book*. New York: Lippincott, 1976.

Index